Should I Like Being the Middle Child?

Discovering Where I Belong

E.T. Elliott

WestBow Press books may be ordered through booksellers or by contacting:

WestBow Press
A Division of Thomas Nelson & Zondervan
1663 Liberty Drive
Bloomington, IN 47403
www.westbowpress.com
1 (866) 928-1240

Because of the dynamic nature of the Internet, any web addresses or links contained in this book may have changed since publication and may no longer be valid. The views expressed in this work are solely those of the author and do not necessarily reflect the views of the publisher, and the publisher hereby disclaims any responsibility for them.

Any people depicted in stock imagery provided by Thinkstock are models, and such images are being used for illustrative purposes only.
Certain stock imagery © Thinkstock.

ISBN: 978-1-5127-9358-1 (sc)
ISBN: 978-1-5127-9357-4 (e)

Library of Congress Control Number: 2017910254

Print information available on the last page.

WestBow Press rev. date: 09/06/2017

WESTBOW
PRESS®
A DIVISION OF THOMAS NELSON
& ZONDERVAN

Should I Like Being the Middle Child?

Discovering Where I Belong

I have an older sister, who
always gets everything
I have a younger brother
who thinks he is a king

I know I should be happy
being the middle child
But why can't I be the oldest
or the baby for a while?

My mom says bread is better

with bologna in between

But why do I feel like the

unwanted lima bean?

Maybe I should leave and
then I'd be alone
I'd be far from the middle,
but I wouldn't be at home

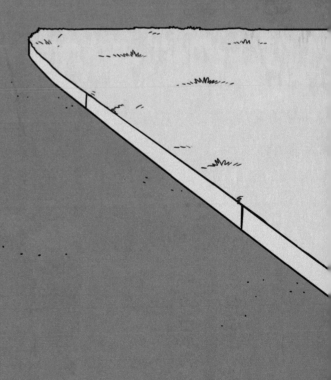

I know mom and dad love
me so maybe they will make
me the only child
But what fun would it be if my
brother and sister weren't around

I wouldn't have my sister
to pick on and annoy

I wouldn't have my brother,

such a rotten boy

From now on I will be happy

being in between

Because with me in the middle, we

make such an awesome team!

Printed in the United States
By Bookmasters